More Than Words

By

Michael Cochran

Scripture quotations, unless otherwise noted, were taken from the (NASB®) New American Standard Bible®, Copyright © 1960, 1971, 1977, 1995 by The Lockman Foundation. Used by permission. All rights reserved. www.lockman.org".

Scripture quotations marked (NIV) are taken from the Holy Bible, New International Version®, NIV®. Copyright © 1973, 1978, 1984, 2011 by Biblica, Inc.™ Used by permission of Zondervan. All rights reserved worldwide. www.zondervan.com The "NIV" and "New International Version" are trademarks registered in the United States Patent and Trademark Office by Biblica, Inc.™

Published by:
Look On Up
Escondido, CA 92026
www.LookOnUp.com

Ordering information, bulk sales, or additional information, please visit our website: www.LookOnUp.com:

Printed in the United States of America

ISBN: 979-8-9865132-0-1

First Edition

14 13 12 11 10 / 10 9 8 7 6 5 4 3 2 1

This Book is Dedicated to my Mom

Thank you for all the hours you have

spent listening patiently to me.

ACKNOWLEDGEMENTS

First off, I thank God for giving me the opportunity to make this book a reality. It is for His glory that this book exists.

Jon Dixon, for turning my writings into a published form. For understanding my goal and delivering such a perfect design for my first book. "I don't understand how to do what you do," but it is excellent.

Judy Bohlig did the initial rough edit and was the first to give some initial feedback.

Darlene Reyes, through her gift of creativity and attention to detail, for editing and giving continuity throughout the pages.

One of the things I found out, while writing this book, is that it is really hard trying to make it through this life alone. My next thank you, acknowledges this. "Truths that Transform" is a ministry at the church I attend. It is also, a ministry I am involved in. Sharon Chapman, Greg Schmid and Diane Geller are the leaders. With these three, it is hard not to learn a little somethin' there. Throughout this process, they have made themselves available to be a sounding board for me. They have read my poems and listened to my ramblings when the challenges appeared.

Thank you.

TESTIMONIALS

This collection of poems allows the reader to understand how God makes each of us a unique creation addressing specific past conflicts, strongholds and life struggles related to the transforming power of Jesus Christ and how He alone can set us free. Michael Cochran evokes feelings of Hope as he shares transparently, his spiritual battles common to the everyday believer or to those searching for God.

As one who has faced these battles and who now ministers to men that have life controlling struggles and addictions of every kind imaginable, I find Michael's open and honest poetic phrases and personal comments incredibly healing as he shares his past struggles juxtaposed with God's love for us that "while we were yet sinners, Christ died for us." (Romans 5:8)

Allan Brenneis
Teen Challenge San Diego

These are the deep thoughts of a man captured and captivated by His Father and His Savior. Thoughts very simply expressed, but very carefully examined and truthfully lived out. Hidden in these verses are the spiritual and emotional "destinations" of Michael Cochran's life and walk with God; "destinations" that all of us visit and go through in various and personal ways in our own journeys.

The "thoughts and intentions" of Michael's heart are revealed here in poetic rhyme, but in everyday language that most everyone will be able to relate to. Above all, one can sense Michael's sincere wish to let these poems minister to others as the Holy Spirit ministered to him while writing them. Many of them "spoke" to me as I read and pondered them. I am sure many others will also find their own connections to Michael's words. I am sure our Lord issaying: "Well done".

Diane Geller
Freedom in Christ Ministries
Emmanuel Faith Church, Escondido

"More Than WORDS" is a uniquely, God inspired, "Play Book," on the role of our emotions.

As a former coach, to be successful in the game of football, you need to follow a play book designed by your head coach. We all experience the highs and lows of our emotions as a result of living in a world full of adversity and celebrations, but many choose to either deny or push those emotions deep within their soul as a result of not fully understanding them.

Michael, using his God given gift through the writing of his poems, has given us context through his real- life experiences and an eternal perspective through God's word. I highly recommend that by reading his book, perspective can be given to your emotions that you may not fully understand. That perspective can then shed light on what we might be feeling, and as a result of that light, we can have HOPE as we put out TRUST in our HEAD Coach.

Dennis Beede

- Former high school and youth coach for 30 years.
- Former high school youth ministry volunteer for 30 years.
- Currently, ministering to at-risk youth, within the San Diego County Juvenile Hall, through The Rock Church, the past six years.
- Currently, Board member of North County Fellowship of Christian Athletes.

It is my privilege to call Mike Cochran my good friend. I have seen Mike's life move from confusion and darkness to light and contentment, all of which is revealed with a refreshing degree of honesty in his poetry. Mike's open admission of past failures make his transformed life through a real relationship with God very believable. His honest reflection portrays a very real human condition with which we all struggle. There is hope portrayed in Mike's poetry that everyone can relate to.

Sharon Chapman
Director, Living Free in Christ at Emmanuel
Faith Community Church, Escondido, CA

Mike's encouraging poetic thoughts of redemption and forgiveness share a journey of freedom in Christ. More Than Words is inspiring, and truly does, "Give God the Glory!"

Darlene Reyes

Over the last 10 years, I have witnessed a transformation in Michael from bitterness to true Freedom in Christ.

Michael has bared his soul to share the way to healing and wholeness in Christ. Through his humility and transparency his poems have given us a road map from brokenness to wholeness in our Abba Father.

Through his repentance and his change of heart he is able to see life from God's eternal perspective.

Michael has been transformed into a man desiring to honor and glorify God. Michael has stepped out of his comfort zone to use his God given gifts to encourage all who are lost or struggling from time to time. Michael, I am so proud to be your brother, I am deeply touched with the life you have laid out before us in your poems. Well done good and faithful servant.

Your brother in Christ,
Greg Schmid

Alphabetical Table Of Contents

Introduction

How do you see yourself? When you are asked this question, do you think of your physical appearance? Do you think about what you do for a living? Do you think about what you do for fun and diversion? These are all natural ways we see ourselves, but do you ever think about how God sees you? Why He made you and what your identity in Him may be? That He loves you and you are His child. That He can't love you anymore than He already does, no matter what you do or what you have done. Right now, some of you may be thinking, "How can God still love me after all that I have done and been through? Some of this by my own doing and some by other's that I had no control over." My answer to this is, He does. God is love. He only knows love. He can't love you any more or any less than He already does. He created you in His image, for His pleasure. Why would He not want the best for you!

Poetry is interpreted by the reader. What it tells you, may not be what it tells someone else. This is the beauty of it, talks to you right where you are at.

The short narrative that follows each poem, tells about what was going on in my head at the time of the writing. I realize that not every poem is for everybody, but my hope is that one of these will capture your heart, right where you are, and give you a comfort that only God can give.

Michael Cochran

How to Use This Book

This book is not just a collection of random poems. It is a collection of thoughts and experiences of a real person. The author uses rhyme. It is his style. It is how his stories come to him. Each poem is about real life and real feelings. Sometimes in a lighthearted loving way and in others not so much. The feelings and emotions depicted in the poems are not unique. Everybody has something in their life that they deal with and find hard, at times, to overcome. Sometimes, just knowing there is another hurting person out there, that is overcoming or has overcome a similar challenge that you may have, can be a comfort.

Each poem has a related bible verse and a brief narrative of the authors thoughts he had while writing the poem. These thoughts may not be your thoughts. That is what this book is all about. Everybody is different. Each person relates to certain things differently. The author has found that a faith in God and a belief in His son Jesus, has changed his life for the better. This belief is what has put him on the journey to overcome the challenges he has experienced in his life.

There is a table of contents that catalog 76 original poems. Each poem has a brief title that tells what the poem may be about to the reader. There is no order in which these poems have been placed. The reader can pick and choose from the table of contents or just start at the beginning and read each in order

The date the poem was written, is included on the poem page Maybe there might be a date that means something to you.

However you may use this book, it is the hope of the author, that whatever or whomever brought you to reading this book, you will overcome and find some peace.

God's Child

I can pour out my soul,
Anytime, anyplace.
You've shown me love,
You've given me grace.

You've told me through love,
I'm a child of God.
And when sins I confess,
The heavens applaud.

You take the broken,
And make them brand new.
You hold them and comfort them,
When they are blue.

On top of all this,
You have given your Son.
Who died in my place,
Now the victory's won.

"But as many as received Him, to them He gave the right to become children of God, even to those who believe in His name, who were born, not of blood, nor of the will of the flesh, nor of the will of man, but of God.".

(John 1: 12-13)

Learning that I am God's child, after all the things that I have done in my life, is the single most important realization I have come to since becoming a Christ follower. Knowing that, through God's grace, I have been forgiven of all my past, present, and future sins. There is nothing I can do to change how God feels about me. He loves me. Always has. Always will.

Back Then

What I do today's not somethin',
I'd a done back then.
I'm completely out of character,
If you knew me, way back when.

Today's a version of myself,
That's grown through tribs and trials.
This life I lead today is one,
That fills my face with smiles.

This life, it keeps me lookin' for,
The goodness in another.
Another traveler on the road,
That I now will call a brother.

So, if you knew me, way back when,
And try to find me once again,
The one you find, no longer is,
Cause God found me, and now I'm His.

*"Therefore if anyone is in Christ, he is a new creature; the old
things passed away, behold, new things have come."*

(2 Corinthians 5:17)

This was a fun one to write. It reminded me of the previous life I had led
and what my life is like now. I don't think anyone that knew me back then
would believe the transformation God has made in my life today. Quite
a difference. I feel blessed and grateful, because of it.

Many Hats

I threw away some hats today,
Yes, I really let them fly.
Most were torn and tattered,
And they cried as they went bye.

They'd been with me forever,
They were like a friend to me,
But now I know by wearing them,
I never would be free.

There was a hat for all I did,
And everyone I knew,
I couldn't have just one hat,
That wasn't safe for me to do.

But living life with one hat,
Would really show you who I am,
And by stepping out in faith like that,
I'd stick my finger in that dam.

It would stop the doubt and worry,

Of showing you the real me,

And begin the real blessing,

The life of love's transparency.

So, I'll just perch that one hat,

Atop my head and take the chance,

That living the way for all to see,

Is truly my romance.

*"And the peace of God, which transcends all understanding,
will guard your hearts and your minds in Christ Jesus."*

(Philippians 4:7) (NIV)

In the day I wore a lot of hats, I wore a hat for the way I acted around those I wanted to please and another hat for those that I really didn't care about. I wore a hat to show you that I was somebody, and another hat to play the victim. I wore so many hats, I forgot which hat I wore the time before. I was embarrassed to let people know the real me. When I let all those hats fly, but one, that is when I started growing closer to God. That was my blessing.

The Fence

The paint was peeling, there was mold,
That fence I sat, was growing old.
The sags in places where I had sat,
"Should I do this, should I do that?"

Or what about those places where,
I saw the footsteps standing there,
The times that I had tried to leap,
Then, after thought, I didn't reap.

I thought of those that I held dear,
While sitting there, amongst my fear.
A fear that truly robbed my life,
That truly cut deep, like a knife.

So, there I sat, and wondered why?
I sat that fence, when I should fly.

"Delight yourself in the Lord; and He will give you the desires of your heart."

(Psalm 37:4)

This poem was one of my earlier attempts at writing. I knew I had some thing to say but wasn't quite sure of myself at the time. I was on the fence between quitting and giving it everything I had. Like most of the poems I write, they are about my thoughts and actions. This one is no exception.

Christ's Friend

Help me Jesus, unconfuse me,
Teach me all I need to know.
Fill me fully with the Spirit,
In Your love I'll surely grow.

Until now my flesh was sinning,
No good deeds had come my way.
But now with Jesus as my savior,
I feel His love with me today.

Each day that passes I grow stronger,
I want to know Him more and more.
The selfish life I've led 'til now,
We've finally kicked right out the door.

Jesus loves me, there's no question,
Loving Him, is what life's about.
I see Him everywhere I wander,
My life with Him, it leaves no doubt.

"I no longer call you servants, because a servant does not know his master's business. Instead, I have called you friends, for everything that I learned from my Father I have made known to you."

(John 15:15) (NIV)

Jesus is my friend? Are you kidding me? When I first heard that statement I was in disbelief. Why would Jesus want a friend, like me? But over time, I got past that thinking and realized He made me to be His friend. He created me in His image, and has loved me from the very first day. I could not have a better friend, than the friend I have in Jesus.

Nothin' On the Table

We do a lot of prayin',
Just the Lord and me,
Tucked back in a corner,
Where no one else can see.

We talk about our families,
Those here and those who've passed,
We do a lot of cryin',
Cause we know that this will last.

Simple prayers between us,
The bond grows stronger every day,
When I leave nothin' on the table,
I find that's the only way.

The only way to freedom,
And to love and peace and joy,
When I leave nothin' on the table,
He's my God and I'm His boy.

*"But you, when you pray, go into your inner room, and close
your door and pray to your Father who is in secret, and your
Father who sees what is done in secret will reward you."*

(Matthew 6:6)

I have been working on having more childlike awe and wonder in
my life. This poem, allowed me to be closer to my Father, by not
holding back. When I am close to my Father, there is no need to hold
back. Why should I hold back? He knows it all anyway.

Help Me!

Can't you see I'm hurting?
I shouldn't need to show you twice.
My eyes they tell the story.
I don't need all your advice.

What I need is, "Who" your love is,
But I'm not sure what to do.
Please help me start my healing.
Why the hell, am I so blue?

I didn't ask to feel this way,
But time's no longer on my side.
What I need is a caring shoulder,
Another's love, to turn the tide.

So, can't you see I'm hurting?
Can't you see I need your love?
Just show me some compassion.
Help my eyes to turn above.

This is a poem about a person who is so close to, "Getting God", they are at their wit's end. It is a cry for help and comfort. This is agonizing to them. They are beyond helping themselves. They desperately need God in their life but can't take that leap alone. They are asking us to help them find, "Who our love is." Of course, our love is God. They just don't know it yet. That is where we come in.

One Man

I can make a difference,
Even though I'm just one man.
By thinking more of others,
And by holding out my hand.

By knowing when to shut my mouth,
And just be there to listen,
When my brother's down and out,
Eyes with tears, that brightly glisten.

Yes, I have opinions,
Some are good and some are bad,
The Holy Spirit helps me,
Sort them out, that makes me glad.

So, knowing that I'm just one man,
Who'd love to right a wrong,
I'll just wait, not hesitate,
When God calls me to be strong.

"For I am confident of this very thing, that He who began a good work in you will perfect it until the day of Christ Jesus."

(Philippians 1:6)

Sometimes I think, "Why bother. What good can I do?" I'm learning I can do plenty. Just lending an ear or a word of encouragement, at the right time, can do wonders. "A well-intentioned hug," can take the place of many words.

Traction

I gotta get some traction,
Trade them deuces for an ace,
Polish that old Cadillac,
Put a smile on my face.

Just because I'm older,
Don't mean it's time to quit.
I still got plenty in the tank,
Life's got no prerequisite.

But sometimes movin' is a chore,
Dependin' on the day.
Or where my mind is playin',
That tries to make it all ok.

I've spent a lifetime playin' games,
With this old head of mine.
Tweakin' this and tweakin' that,
Left for me, no time to dine.

To sit and truly feast upon,
What matters every day,
And have someone to lean upon,
Should I give God that play?

I tried Him once and gave it all,
Believed His Son could help me.
But over time, I felt that I,
Could do better, just to be me.

But be what? As time flew by.
Those wheels throwin' mud.
Just thinkin', sittin',
goin' nowhere,
I had become a dud.

The tippin' point was hoverin',
Right above my head.
It was now or never,
Needed help, or soon
I would be dead.

I ended up submitting,
To the One I'd known before.
For He had never left me.
I, had takin' the wrong door.

"The Lord is near to the brokenhearted, and saves those who are crushed in spirit."

(Psalm 34:18)

Was thinking about getting older. How I can really get in a rut. Everything is a chore. I build up some energy and then sometimes just sit and spin. Like tires in a burnout. Going fast and getting nowhere, until I finally get some traction. This was how my life was going before I asked Jesus to take it over. With Jesus in my life, the rubber meets the road.

Bought

My past is twenty-twenty.
It's the same each time I go.
Nothing new resides there,
And to live there's, not to grow.

Why water what is dead and gone,
When the presence what I see.
I guess it's just that fleeting romance,
Gushing out of me.

God sent His Son to show me,
That my past had kept me bound.
To a journey not yet started,
To a life still tightly wound.

What can I do to change this?
Is there hope for me today?
Or will I sit and take it,
Just believe in yesterday.

But Jesus died and rose again,

With His love I have been bought.

For now, I'm God's beloved,

Praise through Him my major thought.

"Do you not know that your bodies are temples of the Holy Spirit, who is in you, whom you have received from God? You are not your own; you were bought at a price. Therefore, honor God with your bodies."

(1 Corinthians 6:19-20) (NIV)

I was floundering. Past thoughts and memories were my constant companions. I needed a lifeline, and God threw me one through His Son Jesus. What a love for me He has given. To sacrifice His only Son for my salvation. That is quite a price He paid for me. I am pretty special. I belong to God!

Father, Throw Me Down a Blessing

Father, throw me down a blessing,

Help me open up my eyes,

To the fear I see in others,

Who are struggling in their lives.

Father, throw me down a blessing,

A little one will do,

Just, something that will ease their pain,

And show me what to do.

Father, throw me down a blessing,

Don't want to leave this up to chance,

Know that having You beside me,

Might help us change their circumstance.

Father, thank you for that blessing,

You just threw down to me,

The one that shows my purpose,

And the place for me to be.

"Now to Him who is able to do exceeding abundantly beyond all that we ask or think, according to the power that works within us, to Him be the glory in the church and in Christ Jesus to all generations forever and ever. Amen."

(Ephesians 3:20-21)

This poem was originally written in three stanzas. Two stanzas asking God for a blessing and one thanking Him for that blessing. It was originally written in 2020. Today, an additional stanza was added, asking God to throw me down a blessing one more time. There were other words changed also when I realized this prayer was not just for the one struggling, but also for me to be prepared and more aware of what is going on in someone else's life.

Justified

I was lost and Jesus found me,
Through His grace, I'm justified.
No past thoughts, need to undo me,
I'm no longer terrified.

I walk a walk of Him who loves me,
Past regrets and sin no more,
I'm His child and with that I'm joyful,
I'll rest in Him forever more.

What a gift! I don't deserve it,
My former life was not the best.
But His love did not forsake me,
He's covered me, I'm truly blessed.

On top of that I have the Spirit,
Nestled down inside of me.
He waits for me to do the calling,
Then opens eyes, for me to see.

*"Therefore, since we have been justified through faith, we
have peace with God through our Lord Jesus Christ."*
(Romans 5:1) (NIV)

Through Christ I am born again. He is in me and I am in Him. I have
been justified, and I am His alone. Living in Him is a good place to be.

Do a Little Bendin'

I've overstayed my welcome,
Been doin' what I do, too long,
It's made my life quite stagnant,
But I do it to belong.

It's been, "My way or the highway",
Livin' in a day, that's passed,
Tryin' to keep alive, a day gone by,
That was never meant to last.

Bein' straight and rigid,
Keeps me old and makes me slow,
Need to do a little bendin',
Learn some new things, start to grow.

So, Holy Spirit fill me, teach me,
Show me a new way,
That can start me on a new path,
And surely, brighten up my day!

"And I will give them one heart, and put a new spirit within them. And I will take the heart of stone out of their flesh and give them a heart of flesh."

(Ezekiel 11:19)

This one is about me. About my life in construction, and how I have become quite set in my ways. The new kids coming up, have new ways of doing things that don't necessarily jive with the way I learned, 45 years ago. That is a long time to hold on to. In order to get along, I've needed to change some thinking and put into practice some of the loving advice I have received from my wife. A woman's perspective can be quite useful.

Refining Pressure

Thank God for the trials and troubles in life,
For the problems and worries and, oh yes, the strife.
These all have been given to us for our good,
But the world said "nay" and learned as they would.

Now, what I'll say next, you may not agree,
But these trials in life, show us what we can be.
They were given to us by the Lord up above,
To strengthen, refine us, and show us His love.

Problems aren't given, just to those with a past,
Problems abound, but they don't have to last.
Re-think how you think about problems and find,
Drawing closer to Jesus, He'll renew your mind.

So, once we can move towards our problems and see,
That through faith and belief and that we can be free.
Then our load will be lighter and brighter indeed,
cause we've laid it on Jesus, He'll fulfill every need.

"Consider it all joy, my brethren, when you encounter various trials, knowing that the testing of your faith produces endurance. And let endurance have its perfect result, so that you may be perfect and complete, lacking in nothing."

(James 1: 2-4)

"Problems are the refining pressure that strengthens us" I woke this morning feeling grateful and peaceful. It felt strange to me, but in a good way. Life has been filled with problems and challenges lately. Lots going on, and yet, I have this peaceful feeling. I thanked God for this, then wrote this poem.

Christ's Body

We are all in this together,

What kind of awesome thought is that?

When one goes down, we rally,

Strength in numbers' where it's at.

We are forever tied eternally,

We are forever tied to Him.

That makes us all a family.

All together through thick and thin.

No longer are there feelings,

That tell us, "No one truly cares".

They've been replaced by happiness,

There are no more lonely stares.

I'm now a member of Christ's body,

And all the witnesses before.

We stand and sing in triumph,

As we hit that Golden Shore.

46 –Michael Cochran

"Now you are Christ's body
and individually members of it."

(1 Corinthians 12:27)

It is an exciting thought, knowing that I have eternal life with Christ. That I will live eternally with believers, past, present and future, And that right now, at this very moment, I am a member of Christ's body.

Redeemed and Forgiven

You talk to me without a sound,
Then wait for me to hear.
Your patience like a thousand days,
Just waits to draw me near.

Who has that kind of love at hand?
There's only One I know,
His name is Jesus, He's the One,
He makes withered hearts to grow.

For me it hasn't always been,
A life to brag about,
Cause when you've done the things I've done,
That life is full of doubt.

But killing doubt and worry,
Is a job I gave away.
For Jesus gladly took it,
And I'm a grateful soul today.

"For He has rescued us from the dominion of darkness and brought us into the kingdom of the Son he loves, in whom we have redemption, the forgiveness of sins."

(Colossians 1:13-14) (NIV)

What a wonder. To be forgiven of all past, present and future sins. To have all my doubts, worries and fears taken from me. To restore me to the person that God created me to be. This is awesome!

"Better Late Than Never Bro"

"Better late than never bro,"
I heard him say to me,
He'd overheard a conversation,
Between my mom and me.

We were seated at a table,
And he had joined us there,
I was talkin' 'bout the life I'd led,
And how it had left me bare.

For me to see, had taken time,
That Jesus was the Way,
He had changed my life forever,
Because of Him, I had today.

When I talk I use my hands a lot,
And at times can be quite loud,
I guess he just was listening,
He had blotted out the crowd.

–Michael Cochran

I'll always have those five words,
That he said to me that day,
"Better late than never bro,"
Showed me, God's not far away.

"In You, O Lord, I have taken refuge; Let me never be
ashamed; in Your righteousness deliver me."

(Psalm 31:1)

"Better late than never bro." Heard that from a pastor who was sitting at our table during a National Day of Prayer breakfast. I had just finished talking to my mom regarding my salvation and didn't realize that he was listening in. I said something along the lines of all the self-infliction and pain I had caused myself and others, when it dawned on me that by surrendering and letting go of all my victim cards and trusting in Christ, I could have a life worth living, even though I was around 60 years old and felt that it was too late. That is when I heard the words, "better late than never bro." I don't think I will ever forget those words.

"Last, But Not Out"

I got in by a whisker,
But that whisker's all I needed.
I'd lived a life all on my own,
His love, I had not heeded.

I'd heard a thousand times about,
A man whose name was Jesus,
But never cared or trusted Him,
I had no worldly reason.

But there were those that always prayed,
For me, without my knowing,
A case was building year by year,
A reckoning was growing.

That's when I learned my time was short,
I had a chance you'd think,
To contemplate the life I'd led,
But I didn't even blink.

I ended up on life support,
I made no sound or movements,
Just laid there like I'd lived my life,
No obvious improvements.

The day came when they pulled the plug,
To send me on my way,
But something happened, I didn't go,
I was to live another day.

I'd been given mercy,
By a God I didn't know,
He brought me back for one more chance,
This one I did not blow.

"For God so loved the world, that He gave His only begotten Son, that whoever believes in Him should not perish, but have eternal life."

(John 3:16)

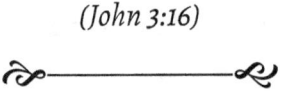

I was thinking about all the people in this world, who have been told about the love of Jesus. For whatever reason, they felt no need for this love. They lived their lives as they saw fit. Our God loves us so much. He wants none of us left behind. But there is only so much He can do. The actual receiving His love is up to us.

"Last, But Not Out", written: 12/11/2020: Page 53

Complete

Listen to the silence,

Early morning, saving grace.

With loving eyes shut tightly,

I thank my God I have a place.

For there I rest in loving arms,

And He calls me His beloved.

Just He and I we start the day,

With no thought of things, I covet.

Our morning prayers together,

Gives me strength to start the day.

Prepares me for the day ahead,

And the pitfalls come what may.

When the light takes over darkness,

As we're walking side by side.

I know my life's complete in Jesus,

In Christ's love I will abide.

"And in Christ you have been brought to fullness.
He is the head over every power and authority."

(Colossians 2:10) (NIV)

I choose to start my day with Jesus. That is when I feel most alive. In that dark and intimate setting, real thoughts come to me. Thoughts of my life and where I am today. How, trusting Jesus with my life, has changed me for the better. With Jesus in my life, I am complete.

When You Think You Got It Covered

"I really blew it Jesus,
I'm embarrassed and ashamed,
Those words came out of nowhere,
Like a Southbound run 'way train."

"I really blew it Jesus,
And I don't know what to do,
I can't take those awful words back,
They are out there and I'm blue."

"I really blew it Jesus,
And this feeling I can't shake,
It's really got me reeling,
And it won't give me a break."

This time I thought I'd made it,
That my life had turned around,
But he came from out of nowhere,
A different game, a different sound.

So, when you think you got it covered,

That's the time you need to know,

That the one who doesn't love you,

Will still try to bring you low.

"Do you see a man who is hasty in his words?
There is more hope for a fool than for him.

(Proverbs 29:20)

This poem came from a place of shame and despair. I had lost it and said things that never should have been said. I didn't take the time to contemplate the consequences. Once those words left my mouth, they could never go back where they came from. They could never be unsaid. They are out there for all eternity.

Rebuild

I sat amid the brokenness,
And viewed what I had done.
I saw a life in shambles,
To me, this life could not be won.

But, somewhere on the outside,
I was able to look in,
And see what life could look like,
If I would let myself begin.

The flame of Truth began to well,
And it warmed me to my core,
The flame became a raging fire,
On its heat, I'd surely soar.

Rebuilding is a process,
That takes vision, strength and tears,
And God, when asked, will bolster us,
And He will wipe away our fears.

"Then I said to them, "You see the trouble we are in: Jerusalem lies in ruins, and its gates have been burned with fire. Come, let us rebuild the wall of Jerusalem, and we will no longer be in disgrace."

(Nehemiah 2:17) (NIV)

In our world there are many natural disasters that happen. People's lives and property are destroyed. When interviewed, the common response is usually, "We will rebuild." This can also hold true for those who have been physically and mentally damaged. I had reached a point in my life, through choices that I had made, where I was that guy sitting amid the ashes. Realizing I was the one who was responsible for this. I imagined myself rising up to full height, covered in ash and grime, towards God's hand that was there to lift me up. No longer, did I need to feel down and out.

Purpose

You made me for a purpose,
Then You gently set me down.
You let me run my own life,
Now I've run it in the ground.

I had to do it my way,
It's the only way I know.
A life without you in it,
Gave me nowhere I could grow.

When I finally hit the bottom,
Where the pain was so intense.
I remembered I had choices,
As I sat upon that fence.

To keep on going like I have,
And do it on my own.
Or love You as You love me,
And no longer be alone.

"For we are God's handiwork, created in Christ Jesus to do good works, which God prepared in advance for us to do."

(Ephesians 2:10) (NIV)

I was created by God for a specific purpose in this life we are living. He made me, loved me and then placed me on this earth. He left in me a hole, that could only be filled by Him. So, I lived my life the best way I knew and in my own strength. Life didn't work out so good for me that way. Fortunately, I asked His Son Jesus into my life. The hole was filled. Also, the purpose He instilled in me, all those years ago, has become quite apparent to me. He has filled me with significance.

Channel Of Life

Cast your cares upon Him,

You're the branch and He's the vine,

The deeper you're connected,

The sweeter is the wine.

The branch is where the fruit grows,

How much fruit? That's up to you.

Cause if your heart's not in it,

Then the pickin's will be few.

For Jesus is the Vine of Life,

His provisions all we need,

He prunes us for abundance,

"Abide in Him," shall be our creed.

So, Jesus, prune us, keep us, love us,

Fatten up that bough.

For that fruit it is a comin',

Our love for You we will avow.

"I am the true vine, and My Father is the vinedresser." "I am the vine, you are the branches; he who abides in Me, and I in him, he bears much fruit; for apart from Me you can do nothing."

(John 15:1, 5)

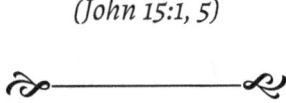

Jesus is our channel of life. Without Him we cannot grow. He is our vine, and we are His branches. We are all grafted to His vine. Without being attached to the Vine of life, we can do nothing.

Cry

What helps you cry, to cleanse you?
Is it people, places, things?
Or is it love or past regrets,
That tug at your heart strings?

We all have different reasons,
That cause that stinging in our eyes,
But the wetness of our tears allows,
Our souls to come alive.

It's freeing and its cleansing,
It wasn't made for just the weak,
It's the way our Father made us,
Helps our lives not feel so bleak.

So, let that flood of reasons loose,
Let them cascade down your face,
Just sit amongst His saving grace,
And know you have a place.

"I will cry to God Most High,
To God who accomplishes all things for me."

(Psalm 57:2)

God has given me a place in His life that has filled me with power and love and a sound mind, but sometimes, I just feel the need for a good, cleansing cry. It brings me closer to my Father, by washing away the impurities of life.This is a pretty good gift.

Satan's Gasoline

I grew up quick, I grew up mean,
I once was Satan's gasoline.
I fueled the fire that he had set,
With sinful thought and no regret.

My sin was deep and firmly rooted,
Foothold to stronghold, it couldn't be booted.
Sin then confession was my daily chore,
Sucked out of me life and so very much more.

This life I was living was causing such grief,
From sun up to sun down, couldn't get no relief.
Then somewhere inside tucked away very deep,
Was the voice of the Father, waking me from my sleep.

He said, "There are those, who clutch at your heart,
They have taken you over, they will not depart."
"Until, you stand upright, and cry out My name,
They will play with your life as if it were a game."

"Now son, take this gift you have freely been given,
And fall on your knees to the One who has risen.
He came down from Heaven with only one thought,
To release you from sin, through His love you've been bought".

"Put on the full armor of God, so that you will be able to stand firm against
the schemes of the devil. For our struggle is not against flesh and blood,
but against the rulers, against the powers, against the world forces of this
darkness, against the spiritual forces of wickedness in the heavenly places."

(Ephesians 6:11-12)

When I realized that I was the one who was behind fueling my sin, I then had a chance, through Christ, to work on eliminating those footholds I had given Satan to rule my life. Whether I realized it or not, I was the one who allowed him to sneak in and wreak havoc. The footholds, over time, had developed into strongholds that became extremely hard for me to overcome. They were deep ruts that I was having difficulty crawling out of. I found Jesus was the answer. With His help, He made a way of escape for me.

Another Year

How 'ya doin' Father?
I'm on my knees again.
Lookin' for those answers,
To those questions deep within.

The ones that keep me up at night,
And runnin' fast all day.
The ones that aren't just cut and dried.
Father, help me find a better way.

So, how 'ya doin' Father?
I hope that you're okay.
Cause we sure need you down here,
To keep those wolves at bay.

A brand new year has started,
The old one passed away.
A lot of us are glad it's gone,
For confusion had its day.

But you're the God that made us,
And when we're honest this we know.
Nothin' happens in this world,
Unless You want it to be so.

"And we know that God causes all things to work together for good to those who love God, to those who are called according to His purpose."

(Romans 8:28)

I like the idea of talking to God as my friend. Bouncing everything off Him. Holding nothing back and asking real questions. Questions that do not necessarily require an answer. Just knowing I can ask Him. Talking to Him because He is my Father and I am His son.

All In

The mirror looked back and asked me:
"Are you all in, or are you posin'?"
Is God your main thought through the day?
Are you a 'Faithful chosen'?"

"Or are you the one who just pretends,
And only goes through the motions?
Ones you hope will get you through,
With the least amount, of potions."

I could only stand bewildered,
Knowing I had been called out.
By someone that I thought I knew,
Now my mind was full of doubt.

When you find you are deceiving,
Not just you, but those you love.
If you're smart, you'll take the high road,
Ask for help from God above.

You know. The One that made you,
Loves you with everything He's got.
Just wants to see you flourish,
Not live with your guts tied in a knot.

What I've just said's not pretty,
May not make me look so good to you.
But after all it's my life,
And now I know what I must do.

Confess it all to Jesus,
Shed my tears beneath the cross.
Give the world back its memories,
And thank God, I'm not a loss.

"I do not sit with deceitful men, nor will I go with pretenders."

(Psalm 26:4)

This is a pretty harsh poem and an even harsher scripture. But when I realized I was deceiving myself and others in certain areas of my life, a dose of strong medicine and confession to my Savior, Jesus, was needed.

Serve

Don't let the fancy things in life,

Work their spell on you,

You're in the world, not of it,

You've got better things to do.

You help out every Sunday,

With the little ones in tow,

You teach that Jesus loves them,

And by loving Him, they'll grow.

Then there are the old folks,

Who've seen a better day.

You spend the time and listen,

As they talk of yesterday.

This is just a few of many,

Things you do each day.

You're storing up your treasures,

Thanking God, you found the Way.

"For we are co-workers in God's service; you are God's field, God's building."

(1 Corinthians 3:9) (NIV)

God has given us an opportunity to make a difference in other people's lives. Doesn't matter the age, who they are or what they do. He puts people in our lives that can benefit from our experience, and their experience in ours. Sometimes through sharing our story, teaching or just lending an ear. There are many ways for us to be a co-worker of God's.

Oaks of Righteousness

Oaks stand strong and weather,
Anything thrown in their way.
With their knowledge of our Maker,
They don't just make it through the day.

They wake from peaceful slumber,
And they thank God, for all He's done.
All the ways He's made life better,
For all the battles He has won.

For turning darkness into light,
And caressing hearts with love.
They stand not on their laurels,
They know their worth is from Above.

And humble is their posture,
As they shake and as they sway,
From all the world's spikes and barbs,
For their strength, comes from the Way.

"...so they will be called oaks of righteousness, The planting of the Lord, that He may be glorified."

(Isaiah 61:3)

Oaks are a symbol of strength for me. They just are. These are people I look up to. People that do. People that get things done, and usually with a smile. When you throw the power of the Holy Spirit in the mix, you have quite a testament for God and His love for us.

Look Up!

I'm so grateful for this day,
And all that it may bring,
Can't wait to get it goin',
Can't wait to do my thing.

For God is always with me,
He's the One that's always there,
His love will never fail me,
He's put me gently in His care.

Just knowing this excites me,
Keeps me craving for that cup,
But if I stumble badly,
I can overcome, by looking Up!

For Up is always out there,
He's the constant I can see,
For when I turn my eyes up,
There's my God smiling down at me.

–Michael Cochran

"I will lift my eyes to the mountains; From where shall my help come?
My help comes from the Lord, Who made heaven and earth.

(Psalm 121:1-2)

Just feeling grateful this morning. It occurred to me, that with a simple movement of my head in the right direction, my current outlook can change for the better. How simple is that?

One Spirit

I'm walking in the brightness,
Haven't been there in a while,
But Jesus took me over,
Started living like God's child.

The way that God intended,
With all His promises to me.
The ones accomplished through surrender,
Then all I had to do was see.

I saw a God who truly loved me,
You know, He made me after all.
To live and be His pleasure,
After answering His call.

So, here I am in brightness,
Feeling love flow over me.
The way that God intended,
For His child's life to be.

"But whomever is united with the Lord is one with Him in spirit.
(1 Corinthians 6:17) (NIV)

I am an electrician by trade. I relate to brightness. It doesn't get much lighter than that. Knowing that I am God's child and will always be united with Him, gives me no reason to feel alone. This is a blessing not to be taken lightly.

God's Word

The Bible is a gift for me,
A book of words to help me be,
The man I was created for,
To bear a load and so much more.

The Holy Spirit reads to me,
And every day's a mystery,
It's full of ways to live my life,
Sometimes with ease, sometimes with strife.

But every way is for my good,
And even though I know I should,
Read The Good Book every day,
There are times when I would rather play.

But then I think and choose the path,
That makes me strong and quells the wrath,
And proves to me that every day,
God's word is where I need to stay.

"For the word of God is living and active and sharper than any two-edged sword, and piercing as far as the division of soul and spirit, of both joints and marrow, and able to judge the thoughts and intentions of the heart."

(Hebrews 4:12)

The Bible is a spiritual book. When I ask the Holy Spirit to show me what He wants me to see, He never disappoints. I could read a verse one day that says one thing and then read it six months later and it will tell me something else. This book is alive, it is God's word, and it is most important.

Wisdom

Is there bitterness on my horizon,
Or am I wise enough to see,
That fearing God completely,
Will make a mortal out of me.

A mortal in the sense that I,
Will run from arrogance,
And believing I have the answers,
Even when they make no sense.

My life 'til now has floundered,
Even though it felt so good,
It's left me feeling empty,
In its place, a heart of wood.

Wisdom has been lacking,
In this life of selfishness,
"Doing it in my own strength,"
Can be no longer, my defense.

So, I'll start at the beginning,

Fear the Lord and trust His way,

Gain knowledge and understanding,

And, be prepared for that First Day.

"The fear of the Lord is the beginning of wisdom: And the knowledge of the Holy One is understanding."

(Proverbs 9:10)

Fearing the Lord is the beginning of knowledge. That is the starting point. It leads to understanding and eventually, wisdom. I have lived my life to this point, with a feeling of immortality. That I would last forever with very few consequences. How arrogant. That kind of thinking has made for a very lonely me.

Adopted By God

You know how to handle me,
After all, I am Your child.
You made me in Your image,
Turned me loose, and I ran wild.

You knew that this would happen,
And let it happen anyway.
My future held the story,
Where my gifts would finally play.

But story upon story,
Just kept building through the years.
There had to be a breaking point,
I had nursed too many fears.

It was at this point You whispered,
"Child, I've come to take you back,
You've learned a lot through all these years,
It's time, to get you back on track."

I then was brought into a family,
With so much love poured out on me.
My life was changed now for the better,
And all my gifts I now could see.

"He predestined us to adoption as sons through Jesus Christ to Himself, according to the kind intention of His will."

(Ephesians 1:5)

Some people "get it" at an early age and keep it their whole life. Others, like myself, must learn it the hard way. I like to call it story building. Experiences, good and bad, make really good stories. My stories come out in rhyme. How do you tell your story?

I Am a Saint

Tender is the mercy and the grace,
You've given me.
A soul that don't deserve it,
But now I'll live eternally.

Because You chose me long ago,
To be with You forever,
All I had to say was yes,
Then worry about it never.

Never live a life of want,
Or question where I stand.
Just give to You my all in all,
That's all that You demand.

I've been adopted, blessed, a saint,
And given all that those things rate,
A ring, the sandals, robe and yes,
A brand-new heart, within my chest!

*"Paul, an apostle of Christ Jesus by the will of God, to the saints
who are at Ephesus, and who are faithful in Christ Jesus."*

(Ephesians 1:1)

When I think of being a saint, I think of the prodigal son. The one who left, rolled around in the mud, and then came back. He expected nothing on his return, but got everything. The ring, the sandals and a robe are vivid in my mind. That is how I picture a saint to look like, and the prodigal son, is how I picture a saint to feel like.

Emotion: Salve for the Soul

I had a thought, it started small,
It barely was a thought at all,
A thought like this I've had before,
It's led to sin and shame and more.

My rebel mind, it needs renewing,
For every day those thoughts keep brewing.
Those thoughts can have a hold on me,
And make my mind a misery.

I trusted God and gave my heart,
But that was just the easy part.
I now know sin is lurking there,
To trip me up and lay me bare.

With all the shame and lust and greed,
It thinks it knows my every need.
I took a chance, I held my ground,
I prayed to God, and this out loud:

"Be gone you enemy of the night,
You no longer have the right,
To take my life and twist it so,
Until I feel that I must go,"

Into a place that makes me cry,
And wish that I could merely die".
I often times wonder where I'd be,
If I had not the Lord in me.

To guide my ways and straight the path,
To smooth the edges and quell the wrath,
That sometimes enters in my mind,
When preparations been denied.

My sin has kept me from a place,
Where God has saved me with His grace.
If I could only let it go
And let abundant power flow.

The life I've only been to dream,
Would dare to give it's offering,
Upon this gift that I've been given,
That lights my life and keeps me driven.

Onward, upward past behind,
My life's worth something this I find.
The love of Jesus in my heart,
This feeling I hope will not depart.

But how I teeter to and fro,
Once I let emotions go,
Upon the whim and will of mine,
With nary thought at all of time.

For 'til I own, the sin I own,
My life will never be,
The abundant life that Jesus gave,
Upon that cross for me.

"And if you give yourself to the hungry and satisfy the desire of the afflicted then your light will rise in darkness, and your gloom will become like midday."

(Isaiah 58:10)

This poem was the first I ever shared in public. It was in a class I was taking at our church. It's a bit long and choppy, but then emotions are not exactly smooth. This poem came from a place of breaking free from confusion. It tells of one man's journey from darkness to light. That one man is me.

Broken

"I'm broken Lord, please fix me,
Put that smile back on my face,
The one that came from knowing,
When You threw me down Your grace."

Why do I keep on breaking?
When I know You're always there.
What is the thing I'm lacking?
"Lord, please show me that You care."

I came to You before I knew,
What broken truly meant,
Now life is showing me a side,
That I can't circumvent.

Until I truly realize,
That broken is a place,
I will not fully understand,
And grow nearer to Your face.

"The Spirit of the Lord God is upon me, because the Lord has anointed me to bring good news to the afflicted; He has sent me to bind up the brokenhearted, to proclaim liberty to captives, and freedom to prisoners; To proclaim the favorable year of the Lord, and the day of vengeance of our God; to comfort all who mourn, to grant those who mourn in Zion, giving them a garland instead of ashes, the oil of gladness instead of mourning, the mantle of praise instead of a spirit of fainting. So they will be called oaks of righteousness, the planting of the Lord, that He may be glorified."

(Isaiah 61:1-3)

Many come to God, because they are broken and know it. Some come to God for a multitude of other reasons. I came to God because I wanted to be fixed and nothing else was working. I kept breaking until I realized that broken isn't fixable. Broke, is a place of submission and obedience to God. It also births gentleness and understanding. Broken is a good place for me to be.

Talk is Cheap

Talk is cheap, so why do I,
Just keep on talkin' more,
And relive all those past wounds,
'Til I'm just a big fat bore.

I've talked so much with others,
'Bout those things that I have done,
When I should have dropped down
On my knees and cried out to Your Son.

Why rehash my grisly past,
Each and every day,
With some poor soul who'd,
Love to tell me, "Please, just go away."

Now crying out to Jesus,
Putting all my faith in Him,
Sounds good, but it's not easy,
Feels like I'm torn, from limb to limb.

"My son, do not reject the discipline of the Lord, or loathe His reproof, for whom the Lord loves, He reproves, even as a father corrects, the son in whom he delights."

(Proverbs 3:11-12)

Wow! This was a rough one. Especially after I read it to my wife. Her response was, "That is one you should read to yourself every day!" Ouch. But she was right. It is amazing how easily I can fall into that trap of "Poor me."

Cleaned Up

Jesus whispered in my ear,
I had finally answered yes.
Then the Holy Spirit came to me,
And took up residence.

This new home that He had entered,
Was no way near a testament,
To all that's good in this world,
You'd have to say it was low rent.

But He dived right in and started,
Cleaning up and making right,
Those filthy rooms I'd lived in,
He turned that darkness into light.

All those sins that I had hid behind,
And that I had tried to make okay.
He cleaned them up, and threw them out,
Now my sin had had its day.

So, I let the Holy Spirit take,
That rusty life I'd led,
and polish it to brilliance, for to Him
I have been wed.

"For through Him we both have our access in one Spirit to the Father."

(Ephesians 2:18)

The Holy Spirit lives inside me. He comforts, teaches and guides me. When I ask and call His name, He is always at the ready. He has shown me how to clean up what is inside and when I have difficulty doing that, He is always there by my side, helping me.

Choice

Let it go before it takes you,
Down that road to ruin.
Not just any twistin' road,
But the one blazed by your doin'.

It doesn't always happen to us,
Cause we're the ones that choose,
To take the left and not the right,
It's "our thoughts", that we abuse.

But my thoughts don't always take me,
To a place that causes pain.
The Holy Spirit's in my life,
He keeps me always in the game.

As long as I keep calling Him,
And thanking Him, for what He's done,
My life will always be with God,
His love will never come undone.

"Who shall separate us from the love of Christ? Shall tribulation, or distress, or persecution, or famine, or nakedness, or peril, or sword?" Just as it is written. 'For Thy sake we are being put to death all day long; We were considered as sheep to be slaughtered.' But in all these things we overwhelmingly conquer through Him, who loved us. For I am convinced that neither death, nor life, nor angels, nor principalities, nor things present, nor things to come, nor powers, nor height, nor depth, nor any other created thing, shall be able to separate us from the love of God, which is in Christ Jesus our Lord."

(Romans 8:35-39)

I was writing this poem, it occurred to me that I was where I was because of choices that I had made. These choices had consequences. Either good ones or bad. Things did not just happen to me, they happened because of me. I also realized that God was always with me. Through thick and thin, His love for me never fails or faulters. His love for me is perfect.

My Life

When it's over, said and done,
And I am laid to rest.
Was my life an open book?
Did I pass the test?

Or was I closed and selfish,
Keeping what I had to give,
Still balled up inside me,
Never really tried to live.

I had a lot to offer,
At least I thought I did,
But I never let it out,
I just sat there, and I hid.

Don't be the one that died within,
And didn't make the choice.
To take what God had gifted him,
And let another hear his voice.

"What use is it, my brethren, if someone says he has faith, but he has no works? Can that faith save him?"

(James 2:14)

I was thinking about the people I come into contact with every day. Do I act and sound like a Christ follower, or do I hide it? Do I use the gifts God has given me, or do I let them be? Do I lift people up with God's words, or do I use my own words to knock them down? These are all good questions I need to think about every day. Life is not easy, but it can be fulfilling if I will use my gifts the way God intended for me to use them.

Give God the Glory

Giving God the glory,
Takes the spotlight off of me,
Puts it on the One deserving,
The One for all to see.

This is the real gift He gave me,
Keeps me grounded, safe, secure,
For if I didn't have this,
My life would surely be a blur.

My success is His success,
That's why He uses me,
To reach the one's in bondage,
Open eyes and help them see.

But in the process, I'm the one,
Who has the most to gain,
For I'm the one my Father used,
To glorify His name.

"Let your light shine before men in such a way that they may see your good works, and glorify your Father who is in heaven."

(Matthew 5:16)

This poem reminds me that everything I have and everything I do, is because God is in my life and in charge. Every success and accolade, I receive, I give right back to Him. This keeps me grounded and in Him.

Exonerated

Maybe just maybe,
I can make it through this day,
And give my angels in heaven,
A rare holiday.

They've been pretty busy,
Chasing me from place to place,
I fear those choices that I've made,
Have put a damper on God's grace.

But they won't ever give up,
No, that isn't what they do,
They'll continue watching my back,
Even when I'm in the stew.

So, I feel they've done their duty,
They kept me safer than I should be,
For, by the wishes of my Father,
He's dropped all charges against me.

"What then shall we say to these things? If God is for us, who is against us? He who did not spare His own Son, but delivered him over for us all, how will He not also with Him freely give us all things? Who will bring a charge against God's elect? God is the one who justifies; who is the one who condemns? Christ Jesus is He who died, yes, rather who was raised, who is at the right hand of God, who also intercedes for us."

(Romans 8:31-34)

The choices I've made and my future choices were on my mind when I wrote this. During my life, I have racked up quite a few charges, and I'm sure, some I didn't even know I had. Through Jesus, God has dropped all charges against me. He has wiped the slate clean!

Hidden With Christ

When I lived life in the open,
There was nowhere I could hide,
Nothing to protect me,
It was one E ticket ride.

I was living fast and wild,
Had forgotten Whose I was,
When thinking's, moving that way,
Things I did, were just because.

That's when I get in trouble,
That's when I start to know,
That I'd put Jesus' love behind,
It left me nowhere I could go.

But I'd let Jesus in my life,
Many years before,
He'd hid me in the Father,
I'd forgotten, closed the door

The way my Father loves me,
Is the Way that I can see.
That though I mess up often,
His arms are there to cover me.

"For you died, and your life is now hidden with Christ in God."

(Colossians 3:3) (NIV)

Jesus loves me. I may fail miserably and lose my way at times, but I know Jesus has me hidden in the Father. I am protected from the evil one, but only if I remember that.

Forgiveness

Forgiveness is a gift that's free,
But only with humility.
For something happed not ours to keep,
Extends our sorrows as we weep.

What could have been a quick, clean cut,
We've turned into a lifelong rut.
"Because he hurt me," is our song,
And many thoughts that don't belong.

To swallow pride and let it go,
Is not as pleasant 'til we know,
The pain was real the pain cut deep,
And left us lying in a heap,
Of sadness, sorrow and despair,
We couldn't see the damage there.

But once forgiveness has been found,
We then can talk of Holy Ground.
That keeps us safe, and in the Hands,
Of The One that walked the Holy Lands.

I run the race to win, you see.

I run the race for victory.

A race of sorrows, hurts and pleasures.

A race of love and joys and treasures.

Quite oft we stumble and may fall,

But realize that all in all,

It's not the winning that takes place,

It's how we finish through God's grace.

Forgiveness is a precious salve,

That gives us hope and lets us have,

The peace once promised and received,

When we said "yes," and then believed.

"And according to the law, one may almost say, all things are cleansed with blood, and without shedding of blood there is no forgiveness."

(Hebrews 9:22)

I found that holding on to something because I had been wronged or taken advantage of only prolonged the agony. Not only was I paying the price for the initial wrong, but I was paying the price again, for not letting it go. I felt that was what I was supposed to do. Not too bright on my end, but letting it go is not an easy thing. We want revenge. We want to see the other guy pay as much or more than we have. I once was told by a pretty smart guy, that while I was fuming and fretting over, "What that guy had done to me," he was probably sitting in front of his television, enjoying a beer and that I was the furthest thing from his mind. That made sense to me. I rest my case.

Simple Words

Simple words speak volumes,
When the heart's prepared to hear.
In times of crisis and of need,
These words can draw me near.

Near to God who made me,
He keeps me gently in His care,
He loves me so intently,
Love like that can strip me bare.

And take me to a better place,
Where the air is fresh and clean,
Where abundance flows completely,
And there's a lack of suffering.

So, with those words I'll listen,
And I will keep them safe and sure.
Securely fastened to my heart,
Through Jesus' love I will endure.

"But thanks be to God, who always leads us in triumph in Christ, and manifests through us the sweet aroma of the knowledge of Him in every place."

(2 Corinthians 2:14)

Simple words between my Father and I give comfort to me. Knowing that He is always there and ready for any conversation and answer any questions I might have. His love has drawn me closer than I ever could have imagined. No matter what I may be going through, whether good or bad, I know God is always near. This comforts me and shows me that I never need to feel alone.

Life

Into the night I fix my gaze,
And think about those happy days,
When as a boy my thoughts ran free,
And told me what my life could be.

But the life I'm chasing now is not,
The life my past thoughts said I ought,
For a Light has entered into me,
And it washes my sin's history.

The sin of selfishness and despair,
I look and simply find it there.
To cast it from my life forever,
And need to think about it never.

Unless I fill this void with love,
And all the blessings from above,
I need to think and stay aware,
Of all the pitfalls lurking there.

That clutch and grab and isolate,
Me from the ones that resonate.
The love and joy that's given me,
A faith for all eternity.

"Set your mind on the things above, not on the things that are on earth."

(Colossians 3:2)

When I was young, I was a happy kid. Nothing was too terrible that it ruined my happy spirit. This carried into my teen years and early adulthood. Then some of the things that I was engaged in started changing the way I looked at life. There was no longer that feeling of excitement. I started finding ways to cover up my inadequacies and failures. This just created more of a downward spiral. Sound familiar? Life has a way of knocking us around. It happens to all of us now and then. That's life.

No Condemnation

There was no way to live up to,
That law that came before.
Just one mistake, a sin, a scrape,
And I would be no more.

Then God came down and saved me,
Using Jesus as His Son,
He lived a sinless life for me,
He died, then rose; I'd won!

I now had a life with Jesus,
No more living hopeless days,
The evil one can't use my past,
To bury me, in sinful ways.

But he sure tries to trip me up,
Any way he can.
But condemnation, will not work,
For Jesus loves me as I am.

"Therefore there is now no condemnation for those who are in Christ Jesus. For the law of the Spirit of life in Christ Jesus has set you free from the law of sin and of death."

(Romans 8:1-2)

I have been saved by Jesus from any condemnation from my past, present and future. What He did for me on that cross took away all my sins. What He did by rising from the dead, took away the evil one's hold over me. I am clean and loved forever by Jesus.

Sealed

Lord, I know; You love me,
I don't doubt that anymore,
I am here to do Your bidding,
It's no longer just a chore.

You've sealed and You've hid me,
It's now safe to walk around,
And pursue this life You gave me,
With a smile, not a frown.

To do what's right, and want to,
Before, was unfamiliar ground,
But now I find it is a pleasure,
Pleasing You, without a sound.

When sealed with God's goodness,
I know that He is always there,
Life, and all that brings me,
I'll still stay firmly in His care.

"Now He who establishes us with you in Christ and anointed us is God, who also sealed us and gave us the Spirit in our hearts as a pledge."

(2 Corinthians 1:21-22)

Knowing that I am sealed by God and have the Holy Spirit as a constant reminder and friend, keeps me secure. I know that God always has my back and is there through thick and thin. I also know that I am free to pursue a life that God created just for me, without that nagging doubt, that once overshadowed God's goodness.

None Of My Business

It's none of my business,

What you think of me,

But it is if I keep it,

And then won't let it be.

The taunts and the lies,

I've allowed to distort,

They've caused me to withdraw,

And I have no retort.

For I've allowed someone,

To take what's not theirs,

And given me doubts,

Through their comments and stares.

Most of these self-inflicted,

For my worth is my need,

Of acceptance and favor,

It's part of my greed.

"Do not give what is holy to dogs, and do not throw your pearls before swine, or they will trample them under their feet, and turn and tear you to pieces."

(Matthew 7:6)

I spent the better part of my life worrying about what others thought of me. Comments, especially derogatory ones, could take me from the highest high to the lowest low, in a matter of seconds. This was a crippling way to live. I allowed another to live my life for me, and it wasn't the life that God intended for me to live. How sick and broken is that? I had allowed my worth to be controlled by someone other than God. I now know this is not God's will for me.

Forward Movement

What can I accomplish,

In a day, a month, a year?

That can move me forward to a goal,

That will push me through my fear.

A fear developed in my mind,

That has kept me from succeeding,

I merely sit and wonder why,

Instead of stopping all that bleeding.

The key is getting started,

And realizing talk is cheap,

For without that forward movement,

It gives no chance for me to reap.

The Father didn't make me,

To live a life of also ran,

Abundance was His promise,

And with His help I'll be the man.

"Blessed is a man who perseveres under trial; for once he has been approved, he will receive the crown of life, which the Lord has promised to those who love Him."

(James 1:12)

Procrastination is a killer. I have struggled with this my whole life. It seems innocent enough to say, "I can do this tomorrow." But, you know, "tomorrow" usually never comes. Everybody has different things that they deal with, but I am finding that I am not the only one who procrastinates. This gives me a little peace knowing I am not the only one. But this thinking does not allow me to get out of my rut. Acknowledging this problem, and that I am the cause, is the first step toward overcoming. I can then take it to God and together we can get to the other side of this.

Take Every Thought Captive

I saw the thought lay dying,

As it laid upon the floor,

This thought had once wreaked havoc,

But we stopped it at the door.

I'd learned that every single thought,

Had only one way in.

One way to disarm me,

And keep me once again in sin.

But The Holy Spirit overcame,

My stubbornness and pride,

He showed me how to catch each thought.

We turned the tide on their free ride.

So I'll just keep on guarding,

My mind from every thought,

And use the love that God gave me,

The love that Jesus bought.

*"We are destroying speculations and every lofty thing
raised up against the knowledge of God, and we are taking
every thought captive to the obedience of Christ."*

(2 Corinthians 10:5)

This poem is about taking every thought captive to the obedience of Christ. Using this verse to stop evil intent from entering our minds and having its way with us. This is one major way that we can fight the spiritual warfare that surrounds us on a daily basis. By calling on Jesus' name, out loud, the Bible tells us that Satan must flee from us (James 4:7). This gives him no chance to get a foothold in our mind. But we must be diligent in our daily preparation.

God's Generosity

God never fails,
His generosity abounds,
When I am down and hurting,
That's when I hear the sounds.

The sounds of heaven moving,
Up above and in my heart,
His beauty is all surrounding,
My soul shall not depart.

With all His love and tenderness,
My strength begins to roar,
Newfound vigor takes me over,
I start the quest to find the Door.

The Door that leads to something,
Bigger, better than myself,
An aperture of Kindness,
Much more powerful than wealth.

The day seems never ending,

When God's love is shed on me,

A love so all consuming,

And it was given for all to see.

"For our citizenship is in heaven, from which also we eagerly wait for a Savior, the Lord Jesus Christ."

(Philippians 3:20)

It is amazing the abundance God lavishes upon us just for being His children. We are also given citizenship in heaven. A home that He has made for us to live for all eternity. This is one more gift God has given us to show how much He loves us and how special we are in His eyes.

Go The Distance

I've spent a good part of my life,
Bein' selfish in my pain.
Runnin' fast and wild,
Hopin' this would stop the rain.

But I found no joy.
No real answer.
Nothin' quite made sense.
I didn't heed that, "Still, small voice",
Found that, that was my offense.

But it sure gave me some stories.
One's that I can share with you.
And maybe help this life of yours,
Not to feel so doggone blue.

When another traveler, bares his soul,
And you are there to listen.
You might hear somethin' in their song,
About that part of you, that's missin'.

That place that God intended,
That was meant for only Him.
The place that we've been searchin' for,
That's been not just some crazy whim.

So, we took our seats and listened,
Found with God, we had a chance.
To live a life eternally.
Jesus had brought us to the dance.

Now the knowledge and the wisdom,
We have gained and taken in.
Needs to find an outlet,
So helpin' others can begin.

For hearin' without doin',
Leaves our purpose in the fray.
And this gift that we've been given,
Will turn to dust and blow away.

"Blessed be the God and Father of our Lord Jesus Christ, the Father of mercies and God of all comfort who comforts us in all our affliction so that we will be able to comfort those who are in any affliction with the comfort with which we ourselves are comforted by God."

(2 Corinthians 1: 3-4)

There is nothing like experience. Unfortunately, some of my experiences came with an expensive price tag. Not all experiences are good. But, on the flipside, these experiences can be shared with others who may be going through the same things I did. If they are willing to listen, it may give them some peace. But it really doesn't matter if they listen or not. What matters is that I have taken some of my hard-earned painful knowledge and became willing to share it with another.

Busyness

Busyness is not a reason,

I will use today.

To cover up my laziness,

To make it all okay.

For that is way too easy,

To blow off, what means the most.

In this I'm truly sorry,

And in this I will not boast.

"Laziness casts into a deep sleep, and an idle man will suffer hunger."

(Proverbs 19:15)

I had started a poem that was intended as a birthday gift. I let life get the best of me and didn't complete it on time. It was almost two months late, and I was trying to find a decent excuse as the reason. This little poem came about through those thoughts.

A Little Stack

When I first tore my wall down,
I still left a little stack,
In case things didn't work out,
The faster I could build it back.

When you first put yourself out there,
And wear emotions on your sleeve,
You are open to derision,
And heartache, as you grieve.

What kind of thinking is this?
I've just set myself up to fail,
And give others the chance to run my life,
I might as well be in jail.

So, I think I'll keep on trudging,
Not looking left or looking right,
Perfect the gift God gave me,
Keep Him close, and hold on tight!

"Trust in the Lord with all your heart, and do not lean on your own understanding. In all your ways acknowledge Him, and He will make your paths straight."

(Proverbs 3:5-6)

Not quite knowing what to expect has held me back numerous times in my life. Letting myself go and do what God has planned for me, has made for some serious excitement in my life.

Where's The Glory?

I'm really in a quandary, Lord,
I've let myself become,
That man that's isolated,
And my mind's a place that's numb.

It took a while to get here,
You know, I really had to fall,
This place that I have landed, Lord,
It's got me feeling pretty small.

I thought I'd done the right things,
Went to church and helped the poor,
Threw some money in the basket,
And had a smile at Your door.

But here I sit quite lonely,
Realizing all these, "good things", I have done,
They were right in my mind only,
I didn't do them through Your Son.

The thought of glorifying You,
Rarely crossed my mind,
I was in it for my glory,
Hoping folks would think I'm kind.

So, I've got it down on paper now,
Where it's staring at my face,
I now thank the Lord Christ Jesus,
For His love and needed grace.

"Let us then approach God's throne of grace with confidence, so that we may receive mercy and find grace to help us in our time of need."

(Hebrews 4:16) (NIV)

Have you ever been down and to the point of brain numbness? Where you come to the realization that some or all of what you do, is for the wrong reasons? That is where I was when I wrote this. I was feeling down at the time. Fortunately for me, I have an outlet through my writing. It helps me "see" what is going on. It is in my face. Sometimes what starts out as a good thing, can end up being the exact opposite of my intentions. We have a friend in Jesus. He always knows all my intentions. I need to include Him in everything I do.

Omniscience

If I were you and looked down,

on this world that You have made,

I would surely be discouraged,

I would surely be dismayed.

But I'm not God, thank you for that,

so, I'll just stay right where I'm at,

and trust that You know what You're doin',

with Your creation bent on ruin.

The world You made for Your own pleasure,

is filled with those who do not treasure,

the love and gentleness You instilled,

to give us joy and keep us filled.

Instead, there are those under Satan's yolk,

who seek destruction, who seek to choke,

the life out of Your chosen one's,

Your chosen daughters, Your chosen sons.

But Your eyes smile as you look,

it's not the end to this great book,

for You are King of this creation,

and Sovereign Lord of our great nation.

"But you will receive power when the Holy Spirit has come upon you; and you shall be my witnesses both in Jerusalem, and in all Judea and Samaria, and even to the remotest part of the earth."

(Acts 1:8)

Just thinking about all the confusion and craziness going on in our world today. It started me thinking about God's feelings. What He must be thinking. I realized that He is in charge and that nothing happens by chance. He is God and He is omniscient. This gives me hope.

Omniscience, written: 3/20/2020: Page 137

Witnesses

I have a group of people,

That I have never met,

Working in my corner,

They won't let me forget.

That sprinkled through the pages,

Of a book that's just for me,

Are the lives of real people,

That lived their life for me to see.

By seeing all their struggles,

I find that mine are not unique,

But they also overcame them,

My life no longer feels so bleak.

They are there for me to learn from,

They took the gift that God had sown,

And lived their lives for others,

Not unlike the life I own.

138 –Michael Cochran

"Therefore, since we have so great a cloud of witnesses surrounding us, let us also lay aside every encumbrance, and the sin which so easily entangles us, and let us run with endurance the race that is set before us."

(Hebrews 12:1)

Being a follower of Christ gives me the opportunity to learn from those who have come before me. It tells their story of overcoming problems in life, not unlike our own. They were no different than you or I. I'm looking forward to meeting them some day.

Smiles

The lines of harshness on my face,

Withdrew and found another place.

Another place to sow their seed,

Their seed of sorrow and of greed.

The lines they found they had to go,

New smiles simply told them so.

When smiles finally find their place,

Their love can gentle any face.

What caused the lines to take the train?

Like rabbits fleeing from the rain.

It's not a what, He is a Who,

His name is Jesus, He died for you.

He died and then He rose again,

And freed us from our mortal sin.

A sin we had no way to lose,

At least no way that we could choose.

But trusting Jesus we found out,

Can turn a sad life inside out.

And start one on a brand-new way,

To conquer each and every day.

"I have been crucified with Christ; and it is no longer I who live, but Christ lives in me; and the life which I now live in the flesh I live by faith in the Son of God who loved me, and gave Himself up for me."

(Galatians 2:20)

A life with Jesus in it tends to make one smile. It did for me. Harsh lines had once ruled the day on my face. Smiles overcame them and caused a gentle demeanor to take their place. Life is better when you're smiling.

God's Temple

God resides within me,
I'm His temple, He's my friend.
I'm His sacred vessel,
This my duty to defend.

We guard against the darkness,
With its evil wicked ways,
That seek to overthrow me,
And to ruin my precious days.

But sometimes, I grow faint of heart,
And my defenses slip,
I tend to fall on comforts past,
And looseness of my lip.

That's when I cry to Jesus,
"I've done wrong, I'm out of sorts,
Please take this feeling from me,
Let You be my first resort."

"Don't you know that you yourselves are God's temple
and that God's Spirit dwells in your midst?"

(1 Corinthians 3:16) (NIV)

God gave me the Holy Spirit as a helper. He lives within me. I don't know about you, but I haven't been a real good host. I need to be reminded that my body is God's temple, and that He is always with me. When I stray, it is because I left. God did not leave me. God never goes anywhere. He loves me.

Home

All I did was say a prayer,
A simple one with no despair.
My life will never be the same,
Cause I'm now a player in God's game.

A game created for me to win,
Even when I'm sidetracked with my sin.
God gave me tools that I carry,
To treat a sin that I can bury.

Not just any sin, "you know",
But that sin that came on long ago.
The one that caused much shame for me,
"Please God, take it, set me free!"

That's when He reached down, took my hand,
And killed the sin of Satan's land.
He told me, "Son, you're now made new",
"And I've got just the place for you!"

"But God, being rich in mercy, because of His great love with which He loved us, even when we were dead in our transgressions, made us alive together with Christ (by grace you have been saved), and raised us up with Him, and seated us with Him in the heavenly places, in Christ Jesus".

(Ephesians 2: 4-6)

When I took my sin to God and trusted in His Son Jesus, I got everything. I became a citizen of heaven seated with Him. All my sins are a distant memory, if I choose to let Jesus take them from me and do with them as He will.

A Battle Within

My life is changing at such a pace,
That I sometimes forget my place,
Where peace and love and joy begin,
Where Jesus died for all my sin.

Yet still I hold to some old ways,
Those ways of old that I still raise,
The big one is the rope that's tied,
To all the past I hold inside.

The past that forever has kept me bound,
To a life I now know is not sound.
The Holy Spirit has come to me,
And has hit me with this constant plea.

"Let go of the rope, and it all goes away,
Those arrows that seek you day after day.
The arrows that life has said is your friend,
But those arrows of life have become a dead end."

"So, let go of that rope, how hard can it be?
A new life awaits you, why can't you see?
By dropping that rope you'll be light as a feather,
No longer a pawn that's been tied to a tether."

"But this rope I've been dragging has become my friend,
It's a part of me now, why must it end."

"Cause this rope you've been dragging is not yours to drag,
Or to boast of, complain of, or wave like a flag.
Is this some kind of a joke, that you use to make light,
Of the life that you've led that you know is not right?"

"But this life I have led is all that I know,
To let go of that now, would be new grass to mow.
I would feel like nothing that I'd ever done,
Was worthy of praise from the Father and Son!"

"Praise from the Father and praise from the Son?
With the life you have led and the things you have done!
Fall on your knees and confess all the wrong,
Then thank Them and praise Them for making you strong!"

So, after that battle had raged in my head,

I uncurled my fingers, and sent to the dead,

That rope that was tied to my past full of sin, And a

new life with the Father, I now, would begin.

"Come to Me all who are weary and heavy-laden, and I will give you rest. Take My yoke upon you, and learn from Me, for I am gentle and humble in heart; and YOU WILL FIND REST FOR YOUR SOULS. For My yoke is easy, and My burden is light."

(Matthew 11: 28-30)

This poem came about one morning when I was thinking about all my battles with the past. All the times I'd failed and tried to make it ok, so I could move on. It turned out to be quite a running dialogue between myself and the Holy Spirit. There have been quite a few of these battles, sometimes not knowing it was His attempt at shaking some sense into me. It was fun to put this exchange into words.

Grace

Life has a story for each one of us,
Did we write it and live it or just make a fuss?
To live life's not easy and sometimes not kind,
But when these things happen, they impact our mind.

Sometimes for the better, sometimes for the worse,
Do we grow from this somehow, or do we just curse?
The latter is easy, it's tried and it's true,
But it's kept us from growing, and that's why we're blue.

We were born to this life with a craving for love,
That could only be filled by the One from above,
He made us, each one to be part of His life,
Then gave us the power to overcome strife.

Now sometimes I win, and then sometimes I lose,
But, to keep moving forward, is the path I will choose,
For, in Christ I am given the free gift of grace,
The grace that was given, when He took my place.

"And He has said to me, "My grace is sufficient for you, for power is perfected in weakness." Most gladly therefore, I will rather boast about my weaknesses, so that the power of Christ may dwell in me."

(2 Corinthians 12:9)

Everybody has a story. Some stories are really exciting and life changing. Other stories, not so much. We have a choice, through God, to create any story we can dream up. We can also take a really bad story and turn it around. This is where God's grace comes in. Through His grace each of us can have the greatest story ever told.

I Didn't Eat That Apple

I didn't eat that apple,
That gave my soul away,
That's filled my life with trials,
Each and every day.

That sin was orchestrated,
By a guy I didn't know,
A guy that lived and had it all,
But it was his to blow.

I didn't eat that apple,
That's made my life this way,
I could have had the garden,
But, what would I have done that day?

I'm sure I would have ate it too,
I'm no different than the rest,
With Satan roaming out there,
He surely would've put me to the test.

–Michael Cochran

So, I have no excuses,

Except the ones within my mind,

The ones that make me feel good,

Where his deception keeps me blind.

"Be of sober spirit, be on the alert. Your adversary, the devil, prowls around like a roaring lion, seeking someone to devour."

(1 Peter 5:8)

Satan is a crafty foe. Though Jesus beat him at the grave, he still roams around finding ways to deceive us and make us ineffective.

Take It to God

You got the vision,
Now write out the dream,
Take it to God,
And make it extreme!

He'll give you the ways,
To make it come true,
But the priority, son,
Needs to be up to you!

Where will you start,
And Who will be there,
To make this dream happen,
"Now get out of that chair!"

The Spirit inside you,
The One that's been patient,
No longer can sit,
And merely just take it.

So, get yourself leverage,

And start up today,

Then take it to God,

And know He'll make a way.

"You are the salt of the earth; but if the salt has become tasteless, how can it be made salty again? It is no longer good for anything, except to be thrown out and trampled under foot by men. You are the light of the world. A city set on a hill cannot be hidden."

(Matthew 5:13-14)

This one came about on a day when I was feeling quite sorry for myself. Nothing was working in my favor, or so I thought. But God wasn't ready to strike me down or make me feel bad, He just started me out with some different thinking about things. Then the Holy Spirit jumped in, and away we went.

Wake Up!

Holy Spirit fill me,
Take my life and kick it up.
Propel me to another level,
Have me craving for that cup!

For my life has been too easy,
And I've lived the status quo,
There is something I've been missing,
Now it's time that I must go.

To leave this life of comfort,
With my head stuck in the sand,
Is not a choice I relish,
But it's the one that You demand.

By asking You to fill me,
And to lead me through the fire,
I've now no reason not to be,
A man, I could admire.

This thought of choosing You today,
Has left me wanting more,
More of Your love and tenderness,
That fills me to my core.

"In whom we have boldness and
confident access through faith in Him."

(Ephesians 3:12)

I have a tendency to get comfortable and let a lot of things slide. I can procrastinate with the best of them. This poem is a cry to the Holy Spirit for a good kick in the pants. I am beginning to learn that through Christ, all things are attainable, and that He can get me moving forward again.

Healing

Talk soft, the people lean in,
Be brash, they pull away.
One way shows you're humble,
The other, doesn't pay.

Talkin' soft and gentle,
That was Jesus' way.
Thousands did surround Him,
On a day, just like today.

Hurtin' people. Everyone,
They heard that He could heal.
Lives of desperate misery,
Had taught them how to feel.

They came by the thousands,
They sat on the hills.
They were hungry for answers,
And the hope He instilled.

He knew they were hurting,
And some still had doubt.
But His reason for teaching,
Showed, what His love was about.

He'd come down as their Savior,
They couldn't do it on their own.
His life He sacrificed for us,
And He did it all alone.

"By this the love of God was manifested in us, that God has sent His only begotten Son into the world so that we might live through Him."

(1 John 4:9)

This poem was written the day after Good Friday. I can't imagine what was going through Jesus' mind He came down from heaven to be one of us, So that we would have a chance for eternal life. He went through this alone, to save us.

Humbled

I'm humbled when I stand alone,
And look up at that sky.
That houses all the stars and moon,
And it makes me wonder why?

Why do we fight and grumble,
At each other every day?
When living in a tranquil world,
Should be the only way.

The way that God intended,
When He made the earth for us,
A place for sons and daughters,
To carry on without a fuss.

And the way we see each other,
Not the way we feel we should,
To help us get along together,
Just like Jesus said we would.

"Teacher which is the great commandment in the Law?" And He said to him, "YOU SHALL LOVE THE LORD YOUR GOD WITH ALL YOUR HEART, AND WITH ALL YOUR SOUL, AND WITH ALL YOUR MIND.' 'This is the great and foremost commandment. 'The second is like it, "YOU SHALL LOVE YOUR NEIGHBOR AS YOURSELF."

(Matthew 22: 36-39)

God created a wonderful world for us. Over time it has changed. But we are still His children and can get along with our neighbor. By looking up at that big old sky long enough we can become small enough to become humble. I can do better by remembering this.

All Things Through Christ

God said I can, so who am I,

To tell Him that I can't.

Saying no to the One who made me,

Would make me look quite ignorant.

But here I am just trying,

To tell Him it's not for me,

And keep up all this crying,

Should just submit and let it be.

But can it be that easy?

Why can't I let it go?

And just become the one He made,

The one He wanted to be so.

He didn't tell me some things,

He told me all things I could do.

As long as I am following,

His strength in me will make me new.

"I can do all things through Him who strengthens me."

(Philippians 4:13)

Wow! In Christ I can do all things. Paul doesn't say some things. Or a few things. He says all things. Because through Christ, I can accomplish anything. I can accomplish anything He wants for me. That is a big deal to me! What am I waiting for?

Let Go of That Dream

Let yourself go,
Now's not the time,
To keep all the good stuff,
Bottled inside.

Those thoughts and those dreams,
You have nurtured for years,
You need to let out,
In spite of your fears.

They are there for a reason,
Don't try to guess why,
Just take it and run,
And believe you will fly.

Fly high to the heavens,
Where God reigns supreme,
After all He's your Maker,
And you are the cream.

Let today be the day,

Where you let yourself go,

Free that super big dream,

Then let God make it grow.

"You did not choose Me, but I chose you, and appointed you, that you would go and bear fruit, and that your fruit would remain, so that whatever you ask of the Father in My name, He may give to you."

(John 15:16))

We all have inside us the ability to bear fruit. Whether we take that ability we have been given and actually bear fruit, is another matter. I was thinking during this poem, of all the opportunities I have had to see thoughts and dreams come true. They never materialized because I became faint of heart at the last minute and did not follow through. These were lost opportunities, given to me by God, to bear fruit. What it came down to, was my inability to trust God enough to believe He had my best interest at heart.

Just Some Guys and Me

It started out as usual,
Just some guys and me,
We heard there might be help for us,
And just came here to see.

With guards up and half listening,
We knew that we could leave,
If topics hit too close to home,
That made it hard to breathe.

We came from different backgrounds,
But there was one thing that we knew,
Each one believed in Jesus,
He was our Saving Glue.

We found that God was not a God,
To always knock us down,
He was the God of grace and love,
Our strength would soon abound.

So, we stuck it out and pondered,
All our deepest, darkest sins,
And learned how we could conquer them,
When love becomes our friend.

Two guys never missed a night,
They came prepared and joined the fight,
A fight they knew they couldn't win,
Without the Love, from deep within.

I may have been the leader,
Just because I'd served the time,
But what I learned from "Just some guys",
I will soon not set aside.

"Iron sharpens iron, so one man sharpens another."

(Proverbs 27:17)

This poem was written about my time in a ministry class at our church. (I am still involved). It talks of getting up the courage to let God work His change in me and learn through the lives of others with like mind. This poem is about how I felt during a class that digs deep. I am sure I am not alone.

Not Mine

There's freedom knowing,
My thoughts aren't chance.
Can create my own,
Life circumstance.

But the one's that enter,
That may not be,
Gifts of love,
Just set them free.

Give them back to,
Whence they came.
Before your mind's,
A hurricane.

Once thought, thoughts,
Were placed in me.
With nothing I could do.

I had no choice,
That I could see.
But with God, that isn't true.

"Wash your heart from evil, O Jerusalem, That you may be saved.
How long will your wicked thoughts lodge within you?"

(Jeremiah 4:14)

Our thoughts don't just happen to us. We have control over what enters our mind. Those thoughts, when stopped at the, "Entry gate," can be turned back from, "Whence they came." God helps us with this when asked.

Unwind

There's a place within my mind,
Where I can go and just unwind.
It's filled with all that I love best,
And helps me forget all the rest.

This hasn't always been the case,
It's taken time to find that place,
For it was buried deep within,
Covered up with years of sin.

Times where I was on my own,
No thinkin' 'bout the life I'd sown,
Just livin' day by wasted day,
And hopin' that I'd find my way.

But hopin' with no work in mind,
Don't give me chances to unwind.
Just turns the screws a little tighter,
Makes it dark, when I'd like it brighter.

So, I think I'll go back to that place,
Where God placed me and showed me grace.
And take the love He freely gave,
After He beat Satan and escaped the grave.

When Jesus beat Satan at the grave, we all won. That one unselfish act saved us all from a life of torment. A life void of the love of God. He built the bridge for us to be with God.

No Fear

Power, love and discipline,
Have got the best of me,
For when I use them ruthlessly.
They kill timidity.

I'm in a battle for my life,
Where fear can take me down,
By using tools, God gave me,
There's no way, that I can drown.

I choose the path been given,
By my Savior and my friend,
Following Jesus' guidelines,
Is a right I will defend.

So, with this newfound power,
I am standing straight and sure,
Even when I'm facing trials,
Through them all, I will endure.

*"For God has not given us a spirit of timidity, but
of power and love and discipline."*

(2 Timothy 1:7)

I look at this poem as a call to action. Paul tells me that my spirit is not fearful! My spirit is filled with power and love and discipline! My spirit can overcome! My spirit takes the high road and never backs down! My spirit loves! My spirit is filled with a discipline beyond self! I am worthy!

This book would not be possible without the love and support of my wife. The following is a little something to let her know how I feel about her.

My Gal

I have a gal that loves me so,

That when I'm wrong, she lets me know.

Sometimes she doesn't even speak,

Just a nod, maybe a wink.

But love is always present there,

Even through that thoughtful stare.

It lets me know that I'm the one,

That she chose over everyone.

www.ingramcontent.com/pod-product-compliance
Lightning Source LLC
Chambersburg PA
CBHW070708130626
46553CB00005B/1891